SCRAP IRONY

Also by Felicia Lamport

MINK ON WEEKDAYS

SCRAP IRONY

FELICIA LAMPORT

DRAWINGS BY
EDWARD GOREY

1961

Houghton Mifflin Company, Boston
The Riverside Press Cambridge

WITH THIS BOOK THE AUTHOR PAYS TRIBUTE
TO VASSAR COLLEGE ON THE OCCASION
OF ITS CENTENNIAL.

Contents

7

MOTHER, MOTHER, ARE YOU ALL THERE?

The after-effects of a mother's neglects
  May spoil her boy's orientation to sex,
But the converse is worse: if she overprotects,
  The pattern of Oedipus wrecks.

FURBEARANCE

"Beginning her fur wardrobe with a moleskin stole designed in high fashion to make up for the modest prestige of the fur, a woman should work her way up to a mink coat just as her husband works himself up to a position to pay for it." From an interview with a prominent New York furrier

From the mole stole
Cut in high style
To the svelte pelt
Takes a vile while
But beguile, smile.

Don't debunk skunk
While your bloke's broke
Add unique chic
With a joke toque
Try raccoon hewn
With a brash dash.
While your dreams stream
Let him stash cash.

When his raise pays
For genteel seal
Keep your eye high
On the real deal
(The refined mind
Will conceal zeal)
Don't digress, press
If he blink, wink
Having thunk "skunk"
Make him think "MINK."

ORBIT

How profoundly analytic
Of his kith and kind
Is the second-rate critic
With the frustrate mind.

A SIGH FOR CYBERNETICS

*Dr. Norbert Wiener, a leader in the use of elec-
tronic brains, warns that computing machines, now
working faster than their inventors, may lead us
to destruction.* News Item

The thinking machines are outwitting their masters,
Menacing humans with ghastly disasters
  As mechanized giants designed for compliance
  Exhibit their open defiance of science
And daily indulge in such gross misdemeanors
That soon they will surely make mincemeat of Wieners.

MINIMAL MAXIMS

The *if* in the gift
Is the motive of the giving.
The *id* of the widow
Adds a certain zest to living.
The *vice* in advice
Is the *I* of the adviser.
The *age* of the sage
Seldom makes him any wiser.
The *lass* under glass
Makes her husband take to drink.
A *cow* in the scow
Makes it sink.

16

LYRIC SUITABLE FOR SNARLING UPON AWAKENING EARLY ON A CERTAIN SUNDAY IN AUTUMN

Rooster with your early crow
   Earsplittingly splendid,
Don't you care or don't you know
   Daylight saving's ended?
   Dawn is now suspended.
If you must be premature
   Can't you keep your distance?
Don't disrupt my dream with your
   Clamorous insistence:
   Let's have coexistence.

Still, suppose the fowl did not
   Agitate his wattle
Baby'd start a counterplot
   Squealing for his bottle:
   Grimly epiglottal.
Tiny tike, why must you pounce
   An hour too soon by clock?
We fed you late, an extra ounce.
   Now, by Dr. Spock,
   Why this poppycock?

IRONIC NOTE, BLACK BORDERED

Though your great-aunt's only merit
Was in letting you inherit,
Volens nolens
Comes condolence.

VARIATIONS LONG AFTER A THEME

I

The race had barely started when the yearling foal
  Began to curl his legs like so much escarole.
The owner asked the trainer as he watched his entry bolt
  How a person could develop such a bad, bad colt.

II

The preacher, Henry Beecher, had a way with wives
  That started whispers buzzing in the scandal hives;
Amazement spread through Brooklyn to the last adult
  That a parson could develop such a bad, bad cult.

III

The Scottish clan was marching to the bagpipes' skirl
  When McPherson's nether garment took a downward swirl.
His clansmen wondered softly as they wrapped him in a quilt
  How McPherson could develop such a bad, bad kilt.

ENCOUNTER

If you've run into a man
Who felt his old Krafft ebbing
    Then you've surely metatarsal
    On a foot with webbing.

PLUMB LINE

*42,400,000 homes in this country now have TV
sets, while only 41,000,000 have bathtubs.* News
Item

Sarnoff welcomes this statistic;
Plumbers, frankly pessimistic,
Feel we're heading down a very doubtful path:
"Do spectaculars and farces
Make men cleaner by catharsis?"
They are asking more in sorrow than in wrath,
And "Can Godfrey, Welk or Como
Bring such sapience to *homo*
As was thrust on Archimedes by his bath?"

SHELL GAIN

*The U.S. Fish and Wildlife Service's Biological
Laboratory has developed a method of protecting
clams and oysters from the depredations of snails
and crabs.* News Item

The quahog cries "Damme!"
Because of the whammy
  Imposed on that chamois-soft clam:
With crabs feeding rife on
His succulent siphon
  He spends his whole life on the lam.
    This makes him feel hopped up
    And all out of kilter,
    So mixed up and chopped up
    He's nearly gefilte.

And what could be moister
Than tears from an oyster
  Attacked by a boisterous snail,
A dastardly selfish
And rotund rake-hell fish
  Who doubles the shellfish travail?
    But mollusks, hold steady:
    Though enemies crave you,
    Your government's ready
    And able to save you.

AXIOM TO GRIND

Vice
Is nice
But a little virtue
Won't hurt you.

CAPSULE PHILOSOPHY

*The psychological effects of space flight cannot be
known, according to Navy psychologists, until a
man is actually in space.* News Item

Can a mere human brain stand the stress and the strain
  That were strictly designed for the birds?
When a man's face to face with remote outer space
  Is he likely to chirp or use words?

Will he hanker and yearn for a rapid return
  To the home of his kith and his kin
Or, when gravity snaps, will this unwonted lapse
  Send him straight to the great lunar bin?

GREATEST SHOW ON EARTH

THE NATIONAL CONVENTION

See the scrimmage and the scrabble
Hear the raucous rabble's babble
    And the ribald rebels' ricocheting roar
While the Chairman pounds his gavel
Trying vainly to unravel
All the barking carking cavil
    On the floor.

Strange, the leaders seem untroubled
Though the hubbub has redoubled
    And the level of the revel is a blast
For the mission, by tradition,
Of the party politician
Is to foster fuss and fission
    To the last.

When at last The Man is chosen
What togetherness then flows in!
    Every enemy becomes a bosom friend.
See the opposition buckle,
Watch the truculent ones truckle;
Under, every man will knuckle
    At the end.

28

THE PLAGUE OF THE LOCUS

The writer who simply works at his desk these days is doomed before he starts; the public has begun to demand originality not in content but in the circumstances of creation. This trend started with Thomas Wolfe's habit of writing on refrigerator tops and really got rolling when Jean Kerr announced that she did her writing in a parked car. While no one wants to go around decrying Wolfe or curtailing Kerr, it is obvious that these two have set an impossible precedent. Few writers can pretend to Wolfe's stature or aspire to Mrs. Kerr's luck in finding parking places. They must either discover new writing methods for themselves or give up all thought of publication.

Several intrepid scriveners have already tackled this problem. The first of these was Basil Benton, a classically oriented young man who decided to write his books in running brooks. The effort was a worthy one, but not notably successful. He started on a slender sensitive volume in April, but a midsummer drought caused all the available brooks to run dry, and Benton perforce as well. Several days of precipitation enabled him to resume work at the end of August, but he was forced to saw his way through chunks of ice before he could complete his last chapter. And when he finally submitted his manuscript, the editors, suspecting that he was engaged in a promotion stunt for an underwater pen company, got cold feet about the whole thing. Benton had already developed chilblains which spread to his brain and killed him.

Donald V. Crandall, a less talented writer than poor Benton but one with a more psychological turn of mind, felt that a technique attuned to the *gestalt* of the times was required.

"The Wolfe-refrigerator Kerr-car axis," he said, "rests securely on identification with the mechanized quotidian aspects of the reader's life." (This sort of thing alone goes a long way in explaining his difficulties in getting published.)

It was Crandall's theory that Wolfe, by misusing an ordinary household appliance, had produced "an attractive dichotomous reaction": on the one hand he invited public respect by imparting new glamour to refrigerator tops ("transmogrification"), and on the other, he permitted the reader to feel amiably superior to the impractical fool who failed to grasp the true purpose of the appliance ("confirmation of the artist-stereotype"). The theory applied equally well to Mrs. Kerr's case; perhaps even better since it also confirmed the deep-rooted public conviction that no woman really knows what a car is for.

Crandall had no difficulty in finding a way to apply his reasoning. The two most logical illogical locations had been pre-empted by the pioneers, but he was quite ready with an alternative: he would write on trains. These, he argued, not only had the necessary qualifications of familiarity and mechanization, but the additional peripheral advantages of suggesting " — of thought," "gravy — " and, in the broadest sense, "wheels going around."

Crandall's experiment began bravely and was chugging along apace until he made the calamitous discovery that the legal cents-per-mile rate bore a relationship to the prevalent cents-per-word scale that made the whole thing impractical. Disheartened but not defeated, he applied to the New York Central, the New York, New Haven and Hartford, and Long Island Railroads for traveling fellowships; they protested that they were themselves in far greater need of grants-in-aid; all parties then filed joint applications with the Ford Foundation, but it will be some months before the results can be known.

In the meantime another writer, Elihu Linot, was attacking the problem from a different angle. It was his contention that this whole trend could and should be repolarized in an editorial direction. "Editors," he said, "need not follow the public as the night the day; they must be induced to *lead* it. The writer truly worth his salt will not stoop to the search for a crass method of creation designed to catch the public eye. He will seek a method that makes an appeal to the editor."

It was certainly a courageous statement, but Linot, after weeks of lucubration, was unable to hit upon a writing surface that embodied sure-fire editorial appeal. Finally, finding himself at a literary cocktail party, he resolved to put the question direct. Cleverly deploying a tray of martinis and two luscious young ladies, he succeeded in cornering a world-famous editor. Once he had managed to make his query audible, the answer shot back, quick as a flash. "My dear fellow, it's simple: just write on the backs of bearer bonds." What with one thing and another, the world-famous editor's enunciation was not entirely distinct; the message reached Linot's ears as: "Write on the backs of barer blondes."

He was, however, enchanted with the idea and lost no time in carrying it out. He was forced to discard the first blonde because she was too ticklish, but the second was admirably restrained and had a splendid broad back. Starting high on her left shoulder with a fine ball-point pen, he was able to complete his first chapter within ten days and the space above a strapless cotton dress. He wrapped the girl in manila paper and sent her to the editor, who telephoned at once to say that he found the work beautifully articulated and would like to see more. Linot's enthusiasm ran high. Working night and day he was able to encompass the next chapter easily within the décolleté of a knitted black bathing suit.

It was then that the blow fell: after reading the text the editor eloped with the manuscript, of which there was no carbon, and wrote Linot curtly that he would horsewhip him if he ever attempted to lay pen on the girl again.

Well, that's where the matter stands to date. It would appear that things have indeed reached a pretty *impasse*.

VICE VERSES

This is not merely a pack of uncurbed doggerel but an attempt to reclaim for the English language the many fine affirmative words that have been lost to it for so long, buried under ponderable prefixes. Now, more than ever before, we need positive thinking couched in positive terms. The time has come to spring to ertia and effect the birth of a de-negation.

HMM . . .

Nothing gives rise to such wild surmise
As the peachable widow with consolate eyes.

37

SOIRÉE

The gentle wives fillet a soul
    Eptly, while the men doze,
Or roast a reputation whole
    On smouldering nuendoes.

SENSICAL SITUATION

Men often pursue in suitable style
The imical girl with the scrutable smile.

SERENITY

The man who wants a quiet life
    And traught, commoded days,
Should find himself an otic wife
    With sipid, centric ways.

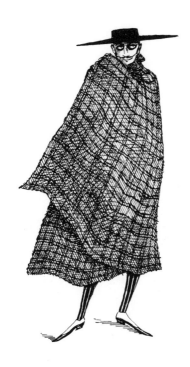

SCREEN STAR

He was known from here to Quito
To both lowly and élite. Oh
   How the populace would gape
When he went abroad cognito
   In his handsome Verness cape!

41

FORMULA

A lady with fortunate formity
  Should dress with a high *colletage*
To foster conditions of normity
  In her masculine entourage.

EVITABLE PLIGHT

If only Jean had never seen
    How far a coat of mink went,
Or if, when winter winds were keen,
    There'd been no men propinquent,
This nocent girl might well have been
    A ruly little linquent.

43

HINT

There never is trouble in finding a spouse
For the ebriated man with the lapidated house.

44

FISCAL FANTASY

Life would be such a nice broglio
  Running so smoothly and mok,
If I had a little portfolio
  Full of negotiable stock.
And if it were tax-exempt,
  I would be gruntled and kempt.

ORGANIC MATTER

He talked about compost and dreamed of manure:
    The veterate kind, nicely rotted.
His acts were advertent, his motives were scure,
    But his wife thought he must be besotted;
His sense of romance was restricted to plants
    (He loved those in beds, not the potted).

He was making things effably hard for his wife;
    She grew thin and perceptibly thinner.
He would clean off her plate with the edge of his knife
    Before she had finished her dinner,
Saying, "Please don't consume it, I'd much rather hume it,"
    He scarce let a morsel get in her.

She finally asked a psychiatrist's help
    Not knowing the analyst spent his
Own leisure time mixing humus with kelp.
    Said the doctor, "Madame, your lament is
Completely absurd. From all that I've heard
    Your husband is just *compost mentis*."

GREGIOUS ERROR

Many a new little life is begot
By the hibited man with the promptu plot.

ROYAL LEMMA

His ministers urged the young monarch to wed,
    But he viewed their proposal askance
When they said that the only girls suitably bred
    Were his nieces and cousins and aunts.
He rejected all these with a touch of impatience:
    "Not one will I have for my queen;
I think it immoral to wed one's relations;
    I much prefer cest — it's so cene."

SEQUITUR

The businessman whose ways are licit
Seldom shows a handsome ficit,
    Never winters in Miami —
    Ah! but friends, his name has famy!

UTTERABLE WISDOM

The wife of a brilliant, becilic professor
   Should never show anity too.
Unless she admits that her brain is the lesser
   Their marriage will never stay skew.

QUILIBRIUM

The iquitous girl often loses her balance
When wooed by a man with unusual chalance.

CRETION

Dora, a daisical damosel,
Was lively and gainly and ert.
　　She should have done well,
　　But the hapless girl fell
For a feeble, fatigable squirt
　　Named Bert.

QUITE FATHOMABLE

A pianist who'd played for the highbrows
    Caused a critical lifting of eyebrows
When he signed with a hillbilly band.
    He explained why he'd taken this stand:

"I loved being veighed for by critics I played for
    But the time had arrived to do things I get paid for.
Night after night I have given my all,
    But I never made much of a Carnegie haul.

"I've played it *andante,* I've played it *con brio,*
    I'll now play it safe with a hillbilly trio.
I'll frankly admit that it's Bach-breaking work,
    But it keeps me pecunious, seemly, and serk."

ASTROUS ENDING

When he clutched his solar plexus
His necrology seemed mote,
But they found his illness fectious
And they cured it with a dote.

TRUISM

A woman's constant souciance
Becomes a dreadful nuisiance.

FINE OLD PROFESSOR

The students who had gnored him
   Universally adored him
And he died beknownst and famous:
   A gnominious gnoramus.

57

NIGHT LIGHT

The sun should not stare at an amorous pair
    With its skance and determined brightness;
It should guarantee shade to a junctive young maid
    Out of ordinate common politeness.

It's rude to intrude on a lady pursued:
    (It inhibits her so in pursuing)
She's always undone by a reckful old sun
    But a feck little moon is her doing.

SARTORIAL NOTE

The maculate lass may inspire a pass
  While she has the advantage of youth,
But if when she's forty she wants to cavort
  She'll be thwarted unless she is couth.

PHILOSOPHICAL OUTBURST

How sidious in tone
Our lives would be
If the *sine qua non*
Were the *cum qua si*.

ELOISE DISCLOSED

Not since the time of Swift and Rabelais has there been as
cleverly disguised a piece of social commentary as the two-
volume work purporting to deal with a child named (signifi-
cantly enough, as we shall presently see) "Eloise." The art of
concealing trenchant analysis under the cloak of alleged
juvenile humor has seldom been practiced with greater dexterity; the cloak has an air of such plausibility that no critic
has yet ventured to peer beneath it. Public response to the
work, however, indicates that there may be a subconscious
understanding of its depth among readers, but this is only an
instinctive reaching-out-toward rather than a true grasping-of
the meaning.

To be sure, it was virtually impossible to recognize the pro-
found and disturbing implications of the first volume until
the appearance of the second provided the necessary clues.
Only then could the petals of allegory be unfolded one by one
until the conception became visible as a whole; only then
could it be seen that the child, Eloise, was actually devised
as a surrogate for The American in Mid-Century, and that
the situation in which the "child" is depicted is the brilliantly
symbolic analysis of Everyman's tragic condition.

The author subtly leads us to the proper mood with the
very title of the second volume (*Eloise in Paris*): the *Eloise
de Paris*, though apparently only a heartrending little anagram
on Eloise in *despair*, also serves to show us the direction
in which the child has been moving throughout the first
volume. Looking back, we find that the whole saga begins
with what we now recognize as a *cri-de-coeur:* "I am Eloise
I am six." In this statement we are at once able to discover

the simple play on words masking the true meaning: "I am sick." Further confirmation, if any were needed, is found in the ending which, with a bit of technical virtuosity reminiscent of Joyce's *Finnegans Wake*, brings the narrative to full circle with a double reiteration of the illness theme, first disguised as a sham sickness ("And Nanny has to get up and pamper me . . . while I am out of my head with fever and pain"), then returning to the original word-play with an added note of pathos: "After all I am only six" (sick). The symbolic child, like her prototype, cannot bring herself to more than a dim, peripheral realization of her condition.

We know, then, of the existence of this illness; but what is its nature? This, as one might suspect, is a more difficult problem in view of the fact that all knowledge of the illness itself is repressed. One must deduce from negative evidence. What, one asks, is the salient *lack* in the luxurious and frenetic life of this child? The answer is at once apparent: she is living *without a mother,* a deprivation made the more poignant by her complete failure to recognize it as such. Yet this is the problem only in its most superficial sense. What is the deeper meaning? Given our understanding of the author's deft sense of word-play, the answer is not hard to find. "Mother" is simply the prosopopoeic adaptation of its synonym, "matrix," and the problem thus exposed is not merely that of a child's unconscious attempt to compensate for the absence of a mother, but of Everyman's desperation in the face of life without a focus, without a matrix.

From this the allegory broadens with ineluctable logic. We have first the child's deeply revealing matutinal rite: "Then I . . . look at the ceiling for awhile and try to think of a way to get a present." To the casual reader, interpreting "present" as "gift," the phrase would seem a puzzling one; the child, having infinite financial credit and the latitude to use it, obviously has no need of gifts. However, following the deeper theme, we realize that this word indicates that Everyman, finding his *present* life untenable, is desperately seeking some alternative to the "nothingness" that surrounds him. (Note here the artful interweaving of the Existentialist theme as in Heidegger's *"Das nichts nichtet"* and Sartre's *"Je suis mon propre néant"*).

Granting the terrible emptiness of life without a matrix, where is our protagonist to turn? This question brings us to the very heart of the author's incisive analysis. We have penetrated the underbrush and are at last in sight of the fundamental point: retroactive tropism. Seen in this light the child's telephonic cathexis is not merely an aimless evasion, but a dynamic and purposeful little ballet of flight. What is it that she seeks when, in every crisis, she turns to the telephone? What does she hope to find at "the end of the line"? It is René, the waiter who, now that we have the key, is obviously her yearning to be *reborn* (*re-né*) into a new and different life. At once the umbilical function of the telephone cord becomes apparent, and the punning conversion of the womb

and its cervical passage into "room service" is so obvious as to approach vulgarity.

Hanging as she is in the limbo between an untenable present and an unfulfillable dream of the past, Eloise (the lost child in everyone) is naturally engaged in a desperate ego-drive, or struggle to find her identity. This theme is rung with delicate changes throughout both volumes, appearing first and most frequently in the reiteration: "It is me Eloise," a pathetic though gallant attempt to create an identity by simple, dogged reassertion.

Paralleling the search for identity we note the faint refrain of Everyman's transcendental aspirations in the "Nanny" figure. This symbol tends to be puzzling until we grasp the fine innuendoes of the deliberate ambiguity. In one respect "Nanny" functions as the superego ("Eloise you cawn't"), yet the clear Trinitarian implication of her propensity for saying "everything three times" marks her as an essentially religious figure. (Has the struggle to reconcile God and Freud ever been more succinctly dramatized?) However, the small amount of security that Nanny offers in this dual capacity is scarcely sufficient to affect the child's *Weltanschauung*, or even to penetrate its hard core of skepticism. Observe the wry neological use of the letters "sk" (as in "sklathe," "skibble," "skidder," etc.) by which even the simplest of actions are colored with the hue of skepticism.

Space unfortunately does not permit a full exploration of the attitude toward the male that is so acidly sketched in these volumes. However, it is in the treatment of the male condition that the author's subjective intensity betrays his (as it must surely be) own sex; and the signature, "Kay Thompson," considered as a chosen pseudonym, hints provocatively for identification with — "Cato's Son."

Yet, illuminating as these various shafts of light may be, one is haunted by the feeling that they all come into focus at a single, as yet undisclosed point, that a magnificent flash still awaits those who have the wit to discover it. But we cannot hope to penetrate the arcanum with ease even now. We must re-examine the original picture of Eloise (Everyman) as we first saw her in the vast lobby of the "Plaza" with its great marble pillars. To this we must add the light of all we have learned of the author's brilliantly devious verbal techniques. At once it occurs to us that, in a work so rich with hidden meanings, this fundamental name, "Eloise," surely cannot be without significance. Yet the flash escapes us still until we think of applying the author's favorite device of letter-jumbling (itself so coruscatingly symbolic of the chaotic state of our times). Then at last the conception entire is presented to us in the dazzling bilingual pun-anagram: OEILLESS IN PLAZA.

65

LOOK BACK IN WONDER

Whom was it wise to eulogize
   And prudent to endorse?
Whose ratiocinations put
   McCart before McHorse?

Who made our state wisconsolate
   And tarnished army brass?
Whose puseyanimosity
   Made egg-heads roll en masse?

Who used advanced roycohnaissance
   And arrant monkeyschines?
Whose merry "Point of order!" chants
   Could curl the stiffest spines?

Who managed to command a spread
   With every news release?
Whose use of propaganda bred
   A million proper geese?

BURIED IN STATE

He wandered lonely as McLeod
  Scott-free of all impurity
Accoutered in a gleaming shroud
  Of clearance for his surety.
His friends were safely disavowed,
  His past sunk in obscurity.
Secure from taint of group or crowd
He worked the furrow he had ploughed,
Alone, immaculate and proud,
But sometimes wondered — not aloud —
  "How guilt-edged is security?"

PETITION FOR REDRESS — 1956

I'm fed to the teeth
With the sheath.
  It hikes when one sits
  Or it splits,
And if one indulges
It bulges.

From neckline to knees
It's a squeeze.
  It demands an eclipse
  Of the hips,
And frazzles, *sic semper*,
The temper.

I'm fed to the teeth
With the sheath.
  It belongs on a knife,
  Not a wife.
A girl needs a breather.
Unsheathe her!

1958
LINES
WRITTEN
ON VIEWING
AN ATTRACTIVE
LADY ACCOUTERED
IN A KNEE-LENGTH
TRAPEZE-STYLE DRESS

When lovely woman stoops —
Oops!

BUDDHISM NOW AND ZEN

Conceptual dichotomy
Had primed me for lobotomy
Until I met a Buddhist fan
        And man!
He really got to me.

Shoot the *dharma*
To me mharma!

BALLADE OF FALLEN IDOLS

Where is the hero of yesterday's quiz,
  He to whom glory was briefly allotted?
Happy the future that was to be his
  Blossoming forth as his winnings were totted.
  "Let him be lavishly mansioned and yachted,"
Worshipers caroled with joy unconfined,
  But finally what did he get? *Sans-culotted,*
Ending the cult of the almanac mind.

What did life hold for the infantile whiz
  Who sprang into fame when his talents were spotted?
Agony twisted his immature phiz,
  Glazed were his eyes, his expression, besotted
  But once people learned that his torment was plotted,
That every grimace had been planned and assigned,
  The milk of their love became sour and clotted
Ending the cult of the almanac mind.

"Who is the chief of police of Cadiz?"
  "Describe every homer the Bambino swatted."
The gentle old lady with hair in a frizz
  Showing no strain on her aging carotid
  Soon got the knottiest questions unknotted.
Legions who wanted to have her enshrined
  Suddenly felt that she should be garotted
Ending the cult of the almanac mind.

Prince, the most exquisite irony is
  That scandal, though leaving our trust undermined,
Resulted in one happy consequence, viz
  Ending the cult of the almanac mind.

74

TELEPHONIC MNEMONIC

Telephone books have become so vast that it strains the wrist to lift them, the eye to scan them, and the patience to handle them. The relatively small compendia of Numbers Most Frequently Called are of use only at home, and not much even there: the telephone company has induced most of us to over-extend ourselves in acquiring extensions with the result that we are always leaving the phone book next to the instrument we used the last time and will not be using the next. Clearly the time has come to develop some sort of system for remembering telephone numbers with a minimum of strain.

The device of *logomorphism* seems the most practical for a word-oriented nation like ours. The game of changing numbers into words has worked admirably for me and endowed me with a splendid reservoir of unexpended time and unexploded temper. Let me offer a few examples to illustrate the technique.

6681 is my own number. For some reason it seems to be difficult to memorize or even to repeat accurately — it usually comes out 6881. It can, however, be immutably fixed by the story of the missionary who went to a small island inhabited only by six cannibals. Nothing further was heard about him until a message was transmitted by drum-semaphor: *six sick; ate one.*

The number 9429 suggests the somewhat exotic mnemonic of a coy German girl with an imperfect command of English who, on being asked for a date answers: *Nein for tonight.* It should be noted for the benefit of those who tend to cavil that the logomorphism need not be perfect; it must only identify the number.

2282 requires that Caesar's death scene be padded by having him identify two old friends among the conspirators before his eye falls on Brutus. Caesar then says: *"Tu, tu, et tu!"* fixing the number with unforgettable drama.

Similar numbers will not necessarily produce related logomorphisms. 2242 is brought to mind not by any connection with Caesar but by invoking the image of a set of Siamese twins who decide to study the ballet and go to a costumer to order the appropriate four-leg-holed garment: a *tutu for two.*

Visual imagery of any kind is most helpful. Consider the number 0415 in the context of a scoutmaster who tries to organize a parade with music, but on finding that his troop is composed exclusively of drummers, cries plaintively: *"O for one fife!"*

Ideally the number should not only be etched on the mind but tied to its particular subscriber, as in the case of a lady who, immediately after her divorce from an extremely unpleasant spouse, was assigned the number 3428, a singularly felicitous comment on her *free, fortunate* state. Equally apropos is the number belonging to an amiable couple who serve delicious food, but never more than one drink, and a weak one at that. To recall their number, 4425, one has only to remember the need to *forefortify* oneself when going to their house for dinner.

Certain numbers seem so startlingly apt that one is moved to wonder whether the telephone company administers some sort of subliminal Rorschach test to subscribers and then matches the numbers to them. Consider the poignant description embodied in 2621, the number of a hypochondriacal acquaintance who takes positive pride in always being *too sick, too wan.*

All of which ought to be enough to introduce the elements of the logomorphic game. It is eminently simple and practical, and remember: any number can play.

LINES ON AN ACHING BROW

I hereby confess
That of all I possess
  I'd most gladly be minus
  The sinus.

83

SPINAL DISCORD

I sing a lay of vertebrae
   Contiguously clacking.
Though once dyspepsia had its day
And bouts of gout held men at bay
   The back is now attacking.

Physicians frisk for ruptured disk
   And spy along the spine,
Discreetly probing every risk.
The castanet of bone is brisk
   Above the patient's whine

As orthopoedic fingers plumb
   What once was loose and limber
From coccyx up to cranium
Till from the lumbar regions come
   The strident cries of "Timber!"

The flying disk and erring bone
   Encased in stiff regalia
Give legions, strangely rigid grown,
The corset's special wheezing tone.
   Ah! Such a bac-can-ail-ia!

INTIMATIONS OF MIDDLE AGE

Work habits slack,
  Nights gay and vinous —
    What can you expect?
    Heaven will object
Launching the attack:
  Pain in the sinous.

Work habits brisk,
  Nights dully tranquil
    Attitudes correct —
    What do you collect?
Slipping of the disk,
  Swelling of the anquil.

Riot of crime
  Or diet of virtue —
    Neither will deflect
    Nature's disrespect.
Once you pass the prime
  Minor parts desertue.

SLIP OF THE LISP

Though a man may be calm as a moose
  At the thought of outliving his use
He rejects, if he's given to truthfulness,
  The idea of outliving his youthfulness.

WORD SANCTUARIES

Some people are born to dictionaries, some achieve them as Confirmation presents, and others have them thrust upon them by schools. Nevertheless, at some time in the lives of most people it becomes necessary actually to choose a dictionary. Often the bright lexicon of one's youth tends to exert an umbilical pull through life. Many a man who has lost his dictionary or worn it to tatters will set out to buy the same one all over again, in the identical edition, if possible; a new type face in his dictionary would be as unsettling to him as a new type of face on his father or mother — probably because, in these uncertain times, so many people look confidently to the dictionary as the last stronghold of immutable authority.

Actually it is nothing of the sort. The modern lexicographer prides himself on being as mutable as mercury and quite as responsive to climatic change. In the jargon of the trade, the approach has changed from "prescriptive" (telling people what language they ought to use) to "descriptive" (recording what language they *do* use). The old rigid corset of correctness has given way to a flexible girdle of usage.

This policy is enunciated in most dictionary introductions, but with approximately the effect of a gnat's scream, possibly because of the small type, but more probably because dictionary jackets, with their claims of supreme authority, persist in implying the opposite. Lexicography may be a philological science to editors, but to publishers it is big business: the most recent edition of the Merriam-Webster unabridged dictionary cost well over a million dollars to bring to market. Usage is a demanding master, and a costly one to serve. Corps of experts are needed to read millions of pages a year, winnowing new words and meanings, noting change or obsolescence in old ones. These readers cover a vast range of newspapers, magazines, and books, marking up a page with symbols until it looks like the bottom of a canary's cage, and then extracting "citation slips" for each context in which each word appears. Other experts monitor the spoken word on radio and television to keep up with current pronunciation. Editors are rigorously guided by these citation slips.

The smallest and newest publishers work mainly with freelance lexicographers. They begin with an out-of-copyright dictionary as a base, or with a word list assembled, according to one candid editor, "by gosh, by golly, and by plagiarism" — this last euphemistically described in the trade as "knowing one's competition." From this point on, editors of large dictionaries and small alike see themselves as devoted and scholarly spaniels, following the path of usage. However, they seem to balk at a number of well-worn turnings. Their image of "correctness" as a concept broad enough to include the consensus of literate error pales before several glaring examples.

Consider the word *jejune,* familiar to many people and defined by 99 per cent of them as "youthfully foolish, naïve," doubtless because of its resemblance to *jeune.* The editors of dictionaries give it only its classic meaning: "meager, scanty, barren, unsatisfying to the mind." *Fey,* construed to mean "elfin" by most literate people, is defined as "fated to die"; its popular meaning has only recently crept into a single dictionary. Confronted with this lag, editors say that the citation slips have not yet shown sufficient evidence to justify the new sense.

There is no mathematical formula for the dictionaries' seal of approval. Editors exercise a judgment based not only on frequency but on range. A word may accumulate a foot-high pile of citation slips, but if it appears only in a single publication it will not make the grade; otherwise *Time* and *Variety* alone could make a shambles ("a slaughterhouse; abattoir") of existing dictionaries. Editors must also be prophets of longevity: slang words often crop out in epidemic proportions only to vanish, leaving no more trace than a measles rash (e.g., *making whoopee, ruptured duck,* and, it is to be hoped, *square* and *cool* used as antonyms).

Dictionary makers must also deal with word coiners who press for the inclusion of their inventions. Their neologisms are often ingenious, but are admitted to the word sanctuaries only through the gate of popular acceptance. The word *humiture,* more succinct and less alarming to Chambers of Commerce than *discomfort index,* was recently submitted to the Merriam Company's scholarly editor, Dr. Philip Gove (Merriam prides itself on its Ph.Diesel-powered staff). Dr. Gove views the word with interest and will watch the citation slips to see if it catches on.

From out in left field (an expression not yet and possibly never to be included in the word-books) has come perennially another pressure on the man behind the thumb-indexing of the brain. Ever since Warren Gamaliel Harding — an unlikely neologist if there ever was one — accidentally added *normalcy* to the language, there has been a rumor that a kind of royal prerogative adheres to any Presidential slip, making it a must for all future dictionaries. "There's nothing to that rumor," one lexicographer says. "If there were, we'd have had to reset half the book for several Presidents I could mention."

Editors are often confronted with pressure to keep words *out* of dictionaries. While they may sympathize with those who campaign against terms with invidious racial or ethnic implications, they maintain that it is their job to report usage, not to change it. Occasionally, however, they slip in a hint of disapproval by defining such terms as "used by prejudiced people." Further pressure for omission comes from the proprietors of trade-marks, who, having spent fortunes making their catchwords familiar, then spend further fortunes trying to prevent them from becoming so generic that they are no longer the sole property of the original holders. *Aspirin, cellophane,* and dozens of other trade names have been popularized right into the public domain. Here again the editors politely disclaim all right to control. They observe, record; perhaps permit themselves a secret smile or grimace.

The idea that a lexicographer is the man who lays down the *lex* is one with strong classic antecedents. In the late sixteenth century, the *Accademia della Crusca* was formed to refine the Italian language and preserve its purity for all time in an official dictionary. The *Académie française* was organized a few years later in France to assure the permanent inviolability of that country's excitable tongue. The effectiveness of these undertakings has been something less than complete: Not long ago, the *New York Times* reported that the 3500 members of *L'Office du Vocabulaire français* had met to consider the alarming pace at which the corruption of the language has been proceeding. English has been creeping in — and not good English, either.

In England the purifying, refining, and smelting movement developed rather more slowly. Most of the early English glossographers devoted themselves to defining the unfamiliar or "hard" words, largely for the benefit of women, children, and foreigners. But the eighteenth century began with a trumpeting of the "prescriptive" note when Swift, writing to the Lord Treasurer "in the name of all the learned and polite persons of the nation," complained of the corruptions, absurdities, and gross improprieties of the language. Remedial action was undertaken by Samuel Johnson, who made no bones about being as prescriptive as R. It was his candid intention not only to stem the current of linguistic change but actually to turn back the stream. The syntax of the fathers was to be visited on the children.

Johnson felt that the language had "spread, under the direction of chance, into wild exuberance" since the days of the Elizabethan writers, whom he considered "the wells of English undefiled." He proposed to cleanse English of its impurities and secure it against future decay by producing a dictionary that would record all "good" words and set a permanent standard for proper diction. Undaunted by the reminder that forty French academicians had labored forty years to produce such a work, Johnson undertook to do the job alone in three ("As three is to sixteen hundred, so is the proportion of an Englishman to a Frenchman"), for fame, the honor of his country, and the unprecedented advance of £1575 from a syndicate of booksellers.

By the time he had finished his great *Dictionary of the English Language,* the three years had stretched to eight, the advance had long since been used up, and he was no longer sanguine about the likelihood of "embalming his language." Yet for the next hundred years Johnson's dictionary was the standard for most Englishmen and many Americans. One Massachusetts judge still uses it exclusively, on the ground that "the language has gone plumb to hell since Johnson."

Most Americans, however, turned from Johnson to Noah Webster, who gave us our first truly American dictionary in 1828. Despite Webster's genius for the clear, concise definition, his dictionary was not notably well received during his life. His price was too steep for the public, his etymologies were too unscientific for the scholars, and his attempts to re-forced to drop many of them. He succeeded in knocking the form spelling met with such frenetic resistance that he was "u" out of such words as *honor* and *color,* in substituting *jail* for *gaol,* and in making many Americans so unsure of whether they were going to the *theater* or the *theatre* that many of them eventually took to the movies; but he failed to popularize *wimen* or to reduce our tongue to a reasonable *tung*. Benjamin Franklin, Theodore Roosevelt, and G. B. Shaw all tried in vain to simplify our spelling. It seems unlikely that our letters will ever achieve happy togetherness with our phonemes: fonetik speling stil haz implikashunz uv unejukatid absurditi.

In 1857, a revolution in dictionary making was launched in England by Dean Richard Chenevix Trench of Westminster. Dr. Trench felt that a dictionary should not be a standard of the language but an inventory, that the lexicographer should be a literary historian, not a critic, and collect not merely the "good" words but all words. His suggestions started the wheels turning on the vast project that resulted, more than seventy years later, in the publication of the Oxford *New English Dictionary*.

The compilers of this lexicon proposed to include every word recorded in the English language since the middle of the thirteenth century, the obsolete as well as the current, giving the full biography of each, illustrating every change in form or meaning by a quotation, proving etymology by the word's history — not by ingenious conjecture, as Webster had done.

This new approach required not just a highly determined man with a quill but a highly financed organization with a staff. The Philological Society sent out a call for collaborators to help with Dr. Trench's proposed "drawing as with a sweepnet over the whole extent of English literature." Before the dictionary was published, over 2000 volunteers were helping in the monumental task. Every parson worth his psalter was busily seining the language and making extractions; literary-minded ladies and gentlemen in England, the United States, and all other English-speaking countries were sending in quotations by the thousand, one man reaching a total of 165,000. When finally completed in 1933, the great thirteen-volume work became the dictionary maker's dictionary and the scholar's delight. One can wander through its acres of quotations with endless pleasure — given the $300 to buy it, the

shelf space to store it, and a back sufficiently free from slipping discs to handle it comfortably.

According to Voltaire, a dictionary without quotations is only a skeleton, but the average or nonscholarly American favors the skeletal in dictionaries. With several hundred of them now on the market, he faces a difficult choice. He is confronted by yards of dictionaries: multilingual, bilingual, encyclopedic, general, and specialized. In the specialized field alone a single publisher, with the resplendent name of Dagobert D. Runes, claims to have published 250 volumes, including dictionaries of Americanisms, folklore, mysticism, psychology, and even tobacco. Narrowing the field to the general English dictionary, there are still some eighty-odd titles, ranging in price from 25 cents to $300, in size from a few ounces to ninety pounds, and in quality from hastily patched-up offsets to fine scholarly works. Yet all of them claim to be the most supremely authoritative, complete, and up-to-date in a given category and to have the most entries with the fullest definitions in the most compact form and the most readable type.

These claims are somewhat puzzling to the prospective buyer. To begin with, he is unlikely to know what an "entry" is (it is any word that appears in boldface type). Nor has he any conception of where a category begins or ends: Is a "desk" dictionary more advanced or less advanced than a "college," bigger or smaller than a "concise"? (The terms are used loosely: the "college" claims roughly 125,000 to 175,000 entries; the "desk" and "concise" are more or less interchangeable, running from 70,000 to 100,000; the "shorter" Oxford is longer than any in this last group. However, as one lexicographer says: "Most dictionary publishers either lie or equivocate in their entry claims: no one is likely to sit down and count." Exaggerations of up to 20 per cent are considered sporting in the trade, but the claim of 100,000 by a dictionary with 50,000 is *infra dig.*)

For some, the name "Webster" might be reassuring if it were not for the tangled web of Websters now in print. The original claim is held by the G. & C. Merriam Company, which bought the unsold copies of Webster's dictionary at his death and popularized it by astute merchandising and scholarly revision. Webster's name was a fertile source of litigation for decades, producing, in some years, more suits than Brooks Brothers. His dictionary is now out of copyright, can be used by any publisher, and is currently in brisk circulation. Merriam and World, the two leading Webster publishers, each cautions the public against confusing "the" authoritative Webster (i.e., its own) with any others. Merriam, somewhat obsessed by the idea of confusion, goes so far in its biographical dictionary as to include under the sketches of Noah and Daniel a warning against confusing *them* with each other.

The Merriam Company tends, on the whole, to exude an air of superiority, perhaps because of its lofty position on the heights of Springfield Massachusetts and dictionary sales charts, but more probably because of its well-merited reputation for consistently fine scholarship. The faint antiseptic aura that occasionally emanates from this company may spring from its ties to Noah Webster, who undertook at one time to bowdlerize the Bible.

The first article of lexicographic faith is that the dictionary should provide the user with the information he wants. Dr. Johnson carried this premise to the extent of listing several words under two headings (*soap, sope; fuel, fewel*), "that those who search for them under either form may not search in vain." The modern lexicographer is too space-bound for such a courtesy, even though it would have spared Clarence Barnhart, the editor of the Thorndike-Barnhart dictionaries, the wrath of a lady who recently wrote in: "There is no excuse for a dictionary the size of yours leaving out a word like 'phsychology'!"

There are necessary limits to the province of the dictionary, but the public, reluctant to recognize them, writes in such questions as: "Does the fire engine, the ambulance, or the mail truck have the right of way?" The editor, if not too busy, will try to oblige (the mail truck has the technical right but never enforces it), but his patience gives out during the mammoth word-puzzle contests. Librarians are equally annoyed by such competitions: during one recent contest the New York Public Library had to call in the police to prevent contestants from frustrating their rivals by tearing relevant pages out of dictionaries.

Editors are also irritated by the practice of selling dictionaries by creating anxiety neuroses ("Are *you* guilty of these common errors?"), or imparting snob appeal to sesquipedalian words. They are articulate and learned men themselves, but they speak with notable simplicity, appearing as anxious as morticians to keep the flavor of their work from creeping into their conversation. They are, however, tolerant of such wordplay as the search for the longest word in the language. According to *The American College Dictionary*'s amiable managing editor, Jess Stein, the old standby *antidisestablish-mentarianism* (28 letters) has been topped by *floccinaucini-hilipilification* (29 letters adding up to "estimation as worthless"), and again by an obscure lung disease, *pneumono-ultramicroscopicsilikovolcanikoniosis* (45), and finally by the one-word description of the spa waters at Bristol, *aqueosalino-calcalinocetaceoaluminosocupreovitriolic* (51), pronounced salutary by an eighteenth-century physician.

Editors prefer to confine such frivolities to publicity releases or supplements; space is too limited in the book itself. Since the public demands encyclopedic material in dictionaries, even the abridged ones include a sprinkling of biographical, geographical and historical nuggets in the main alphabet. The supplements, which are as broadly stocked as drugstores, are likely to include such essentials as: Lists of Proper Names (segregated by sex), Flags of All Nations, Signs and Symbols (from Astronomy to Zodiac), Lists of Colleges (Junior, Senior, and Canadian), Pronouncing Gazetteers, Letter Writing Guides, Tables of Weights and Measures, Population Statistics, Forms of Address (Written and Spoken, from Ambassador to Vice-president), Usage Guides, Glossaries of Foreign Words, Rules of Simplified Spelling, Vocabularies of Rhymes, Alphabets for Semaphoring and Telegraphing, Foreign Alphabets, and the chewing gum left by a visiting child.

To the regret of dictionary makers, the average American demands very little in the way of etymology, and so misses the delights of peeling back layers of meaning.

The *gossip* (*god* + *sib*, as in *sibling*) becomes a full-bodied character when seen first as "a baptismal sponsor," then as "a close friend or chum," only lately reaching the present status of "a tattler." The *cad* is far more interesting historically than face to face, originating as "an unbooked passenger on a coach," becoming "an assistant, as a bricklayer's laborer," shifting to "an omnibus conductor," and finally generalizing into "a fellow of low and vulgar manners." A bland word like *pretty* picks up piquancy when one discovers that it meant "sly" in its infancy, moved on to "clever," and only developed its "beautiful" implications quite late in its history.

Occasional words too lively to sink into obsolescence spring back into action every so often. Dean Trench argued eloquently but in vain for such beauties as *cankerfret* and *wit-wanton;* his list of synonyms for *miser (nudge, curmudgeon, cuff, gripe, pinchpenny, clutchfist, penifather, nipfarthing)* should certainly be hoarded by any word-lover.

The word-lover is generally a mild man, but, like the animal-lover, he can be stung to action by any abuse of his pets. The use of *like* as a conjunction has driven some members of this species to give up cigarettes entirely. Others have committed assault on hearing *literally* used as a kind of double-strength *figuratively* (as in the great blooper, "The pastor was literally the father of his flock"). At such times the emotional word-buff is likely to descend on the dictionary editors, demanding that they abandon their eulogy of usage and return to the good old prescriptive ways. But the sensible logophile simply retires to the nearest dictionary, where he roots about with all the joy of a pig in a truffle field.

LAPSE OF THYME

Of every condiment and herb
    On cookery's escutcheon
    She puts a little touch in;
She throws in bitter, sweet, acerb
Allowing no restraint or curb,
    And when at last she leaves the kitchen,
    Returns to put another smitch in.

To such a cook may fate accord a
Permanent herbaceous boarder.

COOK'S DETOUR

Oh look!
The cook
Who always tests
Capricious
Dishes
On her guests.

She'll skewer
Two or
Three entrails
Adorned
With horned
Imported snails.
Her fey
Entrée
May well combine
Ducks' eggs
With dregs
Of vintage wine,
A slab
Of crab
And powdered mace,
A chic
Young leek
To give it grace.
Her trick
With pick-
Led spinach leaf
Produces
Juices
Past belief.

Her tart
Will start-
Le any eye;
Her past-
Ry's laced
With Rock-and-Rye.

O guest
In quest
Of solid fare!
Beware!
Beware
This cuisinière.

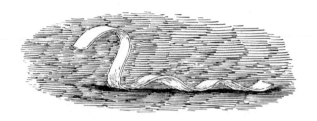

SOUND THE WELKIN, LET THE
NOODLE RING

Seven Chinese noodle manufacturers controlling
the New York Market for egg-roll skin, wonton
skin, suey, and noodles of all kinds, were enjoined
from price-fixing. News Item

That pale mollitudal concoction, the noodle
    Is tarred with the price-fixing taint
But all its adherents insist on its clearance
    From desuetudal restraint.

The trenchermen who delight most in this food'll
    Fight madly with tooth and with claw
If egg-roll and suey and wonton — so chewy! —
    Are caught in the maw of the law.

"Eschewing the noodle is vicissitudal!"
    Its partisans loudly declare
And firmly exclude all suggestions of strudel
    With "Most parvitudal: unfit for a poodle!"
        or "Crude alimentary fare!"

BOTTOMS UP, BABY!

Psychologist suggests small frequent doses of alcohol early in life as a vaccine against alcoholism.
News Item

Baby sows his wild oats with his oatmeal
    Which is laced with a vaccine of rum
And, awaiting his next table d'hôte meal,
    Goes to work on his brandy-soaked thumb.
    What a sober adult he'll become!

He has gin in his milk — just a pony —
    He even has egg in his beer.
Though his bottle would make Mummy stony
    The alcohol-proof little dear
    Is immune. He has nothing to fear.

Baby's feedings are pleasant and fruitful
    For his bottle goes down double quick
And he gurgles while getting his snootful —
    But why does the cute little trick
    Never utter a word except "Hic!"?

OUTRÉE ENTRÉE

How popular the casserole
  So lately called the pot
When serving in the crasser role
  For which it was begot.
A triumph of gastronomy,
  The hostesses will boast,
But is it not economy
  That now supplants the roast?

The casserole can make a pound
  Of beef suffice for ten.
(There's quite enough to go around:
  The guests so soon say, "When.")
Or else it stretches chicken legs
  Until the muscles quiver
By adding giblets, beans and eggs;
  It also strains the liver.

The hostess glows with pretty pride
  And feels she's done her best,
If what she's served has mystified
  The hapless dinner guest.
But he, though splendidly controlled,
  Is thinking, like as not,
"I'm through, until her casseroled
  Acquaintance be forgot!"

PASSIONATE FASHION NOTE

Is there any man maligner
Than the Paris dress designer
  With a fad?
His demeanor toward the bust is
Reminiscent of Procrustes
Yet his lightest word a must is:
  Ironclad.
To lay waist on what was hipbone
He'll cut ligament or chip bone.
  One might add
That he blandly sets his course so
As to rack the female torso
And make husbands plot divorce. O
  What a cad!
  Very Sade.

WOMAN'S WAY

She can master a disaster
    With a fine stiff spine
But her vice in minor crises
    Is the vintage whine.

TREE OF LIFE NIPPED IN BUD

*"TREE OF LIFE, the new sensation lipstick made
with PLACENE, nature's substance rich in proteins, lipids, minerals, humectants and emollients."*
HELENA RUBINSTEIN, Advertisement

She, standing expectant with lips all humectant,
　　Emollient and mineral-rich,
　　Was thoroughly set to bewitch,
When deep in the throes of a passionate pose,
　　Her lover effected a switch:
　　He started to twitch.

Those proteins imbued him with cravings for food
　　He could neither explain nor conceal.
　　As his ardor began to congeal
Her lips, although lipid, seemed strangely insipid.
　　He left — the unchivalrous heel! —
　　To wolf down a meal.

FLOWER BEDLAM

There is nothing I can mention
That exacerbates my tension
   Like the hours
That I've spent in grim alliance
With that gracious art or science:
   Fixing flowers.

Being female presupposes
A facility with roses
   That I lack:
With the rambler or the tea rose
I score monumental zeros
   Every crack.

Fixing gladioli solely
I emerge with an unholy
   Set of quills.
Hyacinths develop bristles
Tulips act like guided missiles;
   Water spills.

Lilacs gird their loins and quarrel
With the peonies or laurel
   In my vase;
Pansies tend to snarl at iris,
Stock to droop as if from virus,
   Phlox decays.

Given total lack of talent
Is persistence truly gallant
   Or just brash?
Though I've fought and died and bled first
My arrangements wind up head first
   In the trash.

SPURIOUS SPRING SONG

Ladies furtively forcing forsythia
   Are always so apt to assume
That they've ended the winter forthwithier
   By fondly fomenting a bloom
     That they venture outside
     With their coats open wide
And return with a blossoming rheum.

BY HENRY JAMES, GULLED, COZENED

Author Winner sat serenely contemplating his novel. His legs, not ill-formed for his years, although concealing the faint cyanic marbling of incipient varicosity under grey socks of the finest lisle, were crossed. He was settled in the fine, solidly-built, cannily (yet never parsimoniously, never niggardly) bargained-for chair that had been his father's, a chair that Author Winner himself was only beginning to think that, in the fullness of time, hope he reasonably might that he would be able (would be possessed of the breadth and the depth) to fill. Hitching up the trousers that had been his father's (tailored from a fabric woven to endure, with a hundred and sixty threads to the inch), he felt a twinge of the sciatica that had been his father's and had come down to him through the jeans. Author Winner was grateful for any resemblance; his father had been a man of unusual qualities: loyal, helpful, friendly, courteous, kind, obedient, cheerful, thrifty, brave, clean and reverent; in the simplest terms: a man of *dharma*.

Author Winner turned a page; his fingers, ten in number, and remarkably, even redundantly uniform (save for the inherent, ineluctable differences of size, shape and function), rested lightly on the margins of pages 458 and 459, having fallen, quite without advertence, into a composition not, as a whole, lacking in grace, yet with each of its separate parts (its distinct — but not unconnected — digits) pointedly emphasizing (indeed, emphatically pointing) to one of the better phrases studding jewel-like, with multiprismatic refractions, the four great paragraphs spread out, deployed, splayed on the facing, the, in a sense, equal but opposite pages before him.

Author Winner said: "Not undistinguished; nor, in all candor, inconsiderable. One might, in fact, go further: Dostoievski would, as a sentient man, have been forced, though not without a tinge of viridity, to cry: 'Хорошо!' And Joyce?"

Author Winner shrugged faintly, allowing the question to hang, for a moment, in the air (that brave o'erhanging firmament!) above his head; his eyes, rubescent from exposure to the wind in his bellying sales, narrowed. *Re* Joyce: could any reasonable man pretend (without hypocrisy) to know what Joyce would have thought — or indeed what, ultimately or, for that matter, penultimately, he, in his anfractuosity, *did* think? The answer was pellucidly clear: No! One could not profitably spend one's time *re-Joycing*.

Hearing the sound of a key in the latch, Author Winner, with not-unceremonious decorum, rose, his well-tailored jacket sagging slightly from the weight of all the critics in his pocket, *nemine dissentiente.*

Bouncing in on sturdy feet, encased in fulgent shoes of cordovan leather, was his wife, Clarifier, her arms, although long and well-muscled, encumbered with packages. Of her burdens relieving her (an act he performed habitually, indeed, instinctively in all personal relations), Author Winner, with eloquent simplicity, said: "Hello."

Clarifier, with a faint (leporine) vellication of her nose (a tic Author Winner found at once repellent and subtly attractive), removed her hat. She said: "Darling, I venture to say that you, with your ever-probing intelligence, will deduce that I've been out."

Author Winner said: "I will; I, in fact, have."

Clarifier, removing her coat and turning to suspend it in the well-constructed wardrobe that had been her father's-in-law (himself defunct while this relationship was still uneventuate), revealing a nascent tendency toward steatopygia, permitted a paper to flutter from her pocket, the which Author Winner stooped (his inherent grace negating the implicit onus of the act) to retrieve.

Clarifier heartily said: "Oh, the milk bill. I had intended to give it to you, darling, before I departed from our residence at 10:08 this A.M."

Author Winner went to his desk; he was a man who liked to settle his accounts promptly, his ancestors on both sides having been early settlers.

Following him with springy steps Clarifier said: "We have, darling, a new milkman. Noting that he appeared ignorant concerning us, I invited him in for a cup of instant coffee and ventured to inform him that you, although an Author born, had only recently become an in-the-fullest-sense Winner, that I, following a chance encounter at the home of your germane cousin, Claude, and a courtship of four and a half months, became your wife in a church ceremony, and that we were, now as then, childless."

Author Winner said: "What manner of man is this purveyor of milk?"

Clarifier said: "I'm glad, darling, that you asked that question; he is, as I myself discovered, a most-interesting combination. His mother was half Negro and half Jewish; his father, Catholic and Episcopalian in equal parts."

Frowning, Author Winner said: "I trust you entertained the Episcopalian part only."

It was then that the storm broke: the inevitable effect of the fortuitous concatenation of air currents and pressure areas; raging electrically, symbolically, above and on the four sides of the house, it was nevertheless able to exercise (intent upon exercising!) a subtle penetration. Author Winner and his wife, responding to a common (deep-rooted) impulse, found themselves moving toward the living-room windows, left open (no! intentionally raised some hours before against the matutinal calidity), and now admitting the (inadmissible) humectation. Together closing, then standing for a moment in the resultant closeness, they found themselves (together still!) mounting, mounting! And then, a fumbling to open (the distaff distrait), superseded by Author Winner's deft dexterity; a brief interval of exploration, and then — the moment of revelation: His, and then Hers, Hers, Hers, and again and again Hers! in rapid succession, until Clarifier, sensing her husband's discomfiture, shyly said: "There was a white sale at Macy's; the Hers towels were half-price."

From the second-floor bedroom descended (with the instinctive dignity of a man descending from Charlemagne), in his chair once more settled, Author Winner, collecting himself in tranquillity, again looked upon his work and found it good. (Not by my syntax wilt thou judge me!) But was it perfect? It was this question that he had set himself sincerely to answer (One self-approving hour whole years outweighs Of stupid starers and of loud huzzas); as a Man of Reason, his impulse (itself a distillation of reason and his deeply-probing, deeply-boring knowledge of the science of probabilities that would the late J. M. Keynes have put to shame) had been: Perhaps not. But *if* not perfect, then, as a Man of Reason (that man that is not passion's slave!), *how* not? Eluding him still was the answer, if answer there were; the question itself hung (as no jury in the land could be persuaded to do, the verdict being, one might say, already in the "bag": *nemo me impune lacessit*) burning, as it were, suffusing the very atmosphere.

Clarifier, her healthy yet salicional voice preceding her down the stairs, said: "Oh, darling, the custard has boiled over! I reproach myself with my failure to watch it more closely; but, this being Thursday, Agatha, our 'help,' is 'off,' and I had, as you know, no knowledge of the domestic arts prior to our marriage seven years ago."

Author Winner wryly said: "*Quis custodiet istos* custard?" Not uncondign was her smiling gratitude as Author Winner, tightening his belt and shortening his suspenders, rose (as he invariably did to an occasion), and accompanied her to the kitchen.

Clarifier said: "There is a thing I must communicate to you, darling. Pausing for a moment in the street to pass the time of

day with Rufus L. Cutler, our competent though erratic family splanchnologist, I neglected to note that I had parked under a bridge. In that brief moment I was with a parking ticket slapped."

Author Winner said: "The law, in its majestic equality, forbids the rich as well as the poor to park under bridges."

Clarifier said: "Yes, darling, but how can I get the ticket fixed? I have no wish to pay a five-dollar fine."

Author Winner said: "Listen to me closely: Estoppel, whether equitable or in pais, arises upon doctrine that relevant evidence, having probative value, is prima facie admissible; relief or remedial provisions of statute must be liberally construed to effectuate the objective prospectively and not retroactively; moreover, jurisdiction cannot be conferred by agreement, consent or collusion, nor can parties be precluded from raising question by any form of laches or waiver. Is that perfectly clear, my dear?"

Clarifier gratefully said: "Oh, perfectly, darling! Could you just give me five dollars which I require for certain minor domestic expenses?"

Of the five dollars possessed, she, with not-unaccustomed softness, Author Winner having already resumed, with resolute concentration, the labors on which he had previously been engaged, tiptoed from the room. Author Winner, his mind irenic, his body composed, despite the dissipation of thought attendant on the interruption (the noble dust of Alexander stopping a bung-hole!), marshalled and polarized his not-inconsiderable faculties. Could it (veridically) be said that there was in the work before him any lacuna, omission, wantage, ullage, insufficiency? It could not! The conception was (*troppo disputare la verità fa errore*) magnificent: the middle-aged man in the middle-sized town; he, at the moment of his maximal wing-spread caught, it, by its ultimate perimeter circumscribed; the whole including all that was truly American — all!: alcoholism, bastardy, criminality, digamy, embezzlement, fornication — but here, surely, the compendior must pause in his à-corps-perdu alphabetical march to wonder at the courageous and varied treatment accorded this subject in all its forms, aspects, manifestations and classifications (more things in heaven and earth, Krafft-Ebing, than are dreamed of in your philosophy!). Sex, with the clinical eye, fixed, with the lyrical pen, transfixed; sex somnifacient! Pederasty, lightly limned (yet deftly, penetratingly): the organist disorganized, implicitly, as it were, disorganed (O! the irony in the velvet glove!); the scanty pinch of scatology to titillate the caprophilist in every critic — But why continue? The work was indeed complete, exhaustive, plenary, consummate.

And of contemporary competition there was blatantly none: he had, with negligent ease, put in her painful place that one who had dared to aspire to his primacy (though not yet his in fact, still his in palpable incipience), transmogrifying the base metalios with his philosopher's stone; he had, in following two masters of style, outmastered them both, meandering with the one, yet avoiding the catafalknerian pall, outinvoluting the other to the oxymoronic point of sheer opacity.

Author Winner, having examined the question oxybleptically, and having plucked out of this nettle, the flower, was able, at last, to sink back in his chair content. His foundation was secure, and upon it he had builded better than he knew.

At this moment, with a brief, succusive movement, the chair that had been his father's (built for sempiternity!) crumbled beneath Author Winner, disintegrating, comminuting in a flash! He, for a moment only vacillating, then renitent, inflexible, maintained his position: spine held vertical at 96 degree angle to femur, tibia at right angles to femur and floor. Author Winner thought: I must be Reasonable. Yet, deprived of all support, what is now the reasonable thing to do? Collapse? Never; not at any time! Rigid, rigidifying he thought: I-I-I have the strength!

Clarifier, entering then, seeing with her slightly-exophthalmic eyes the obvious, rushed to fetch a kitchen stool, which,

returning, she inserted beneath (beneath!) Author Winner.
Could he to descend to this shoddy, this crass, this lowest-of-
possible supports bring himself?

Diamantine, unyielding, he said: "I am higher."

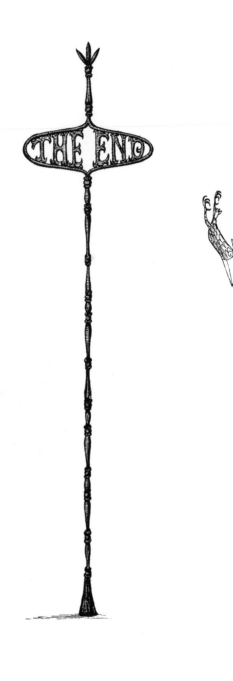